Indie Writing Advice

By Denice Shaw

Indie Writing Advice: A Simple Guide on Writing and Optimizing Your Social Media Platform

I've been writing for nearly a decade, and I can honestly say that becoming a writer has been the most challenging, rewarding, life changing and thought provoking experience for me to date.

Becoming a writer was not an overnight decision. I began with a memoir and thought that would be it. Until another memoir idea came to mind. Then a storyline literally popped into my head out of the blue one morning, and I wrote my first romantic mystery.

You see a pattern here?

Some people are born writers; while others have it in the back of their mind for a long time and then one day the story ideas can no longer be suppressed. The latter is obviously the case for me.

But today it isn't enough just to be a writer; there's a lot more to it and that is what this book is about. In this book you'll find simple, easy to follow steps to help you make the most out of your platform and your writing. I hope you find my input useful and motivating. All the best of luck to you!

What you'll find in this book:

-Being a writer is easy, right?
-Your first book, is it all about ego?
-Subsidy publishing; friend or foe?
-Character development: letting your baby go
-Let your readers fall in love with your character, not your plot
-Tips on how to write an honest book review
-How to write a crappy book
-10 common mistakes made in your first draft
-Do you like weak blogs or strong blogs?
-If you wouldn't read it to your mother, would you read it yourself?
-15 Tips for the First Day of Your KDP Select FREE Promotion
-5 More Tips to Make the Best out of Your KDP Select FREE Promotion Days
-My Kindle FREE promotion is over....now what?

Being a Writer is Easy, Right?

Someone asked, "Being a writer is easy, right?" not long ago, and I wasn't sure if it was a joke. My response was tongue in cheek, "Oh yeah, you work 60 hours a week and get paid in likes, comments and shares….sure, it's easy work." I waved.

If it was easy, everyone would be successful at it, right? Let's face it, there are many writers out there, but there are also many unsuccessful writers. Just like any profession. The trouble is, most writers don't even get to make through the door. We have our book, our baby, in hand. We've poured months, if not years of our lives into our first masterpiece, only to have the door slammed in our face.

When you finally have your manuscript completed, you haven't even scratched the surface.

I had this conversation with a young man a short time ago. He'd written a novel during high school a few years back, and he sent it to one publisher who rejected it. He burned his original manuscript in protest.

Most people assume that being a writer is just about writing books, hitting the best seller list and kicking back.

If you want a career that tests your patience….be a writer.

After you've written your heart out on paper, then you have to worry about beta readers, editors and reviewers. Then the burning question:

Do I send query letters to agents and publishers, or do I self publish?

That is the question that's been on my mind since my first book, and I think this is where the problem lies. If you do it properly and follow through with the steps (beta readers, editors, reviewers), make your manuscript the best it can be, and THEN send it to agents and publishers, some writers MIGHT have a chance.

I think this is what's going wrong in the publishing world. Too many people are skipping all these important steps and either sending to publishers/agents or self publishing immediately after their first draft. Perhaps **trying to make a fast buck?** So the bottleneck effect happens at the publishing stage.

Then, once you've arrived at the decision to self publish, you have to research WHERE.

You need to have your book available in as many formats and as many platforms as possible. DO NOT LIMIT YOURSELF!! We all know the big ones are Amazon and Smashwords. But we STILL haven't even scratched the surface. Are you still with me?

Next, you have to worry about marketing. HOW do I get my book seen? Everyone knows the two biggest and best ways are through BLOGGING and SOCIAL MEDIA. Do you want to laugh? <u>You have to have your social platform established BEFORE you get to this step!</u> Yes! No jokes! Banging your head against the wall yet?
<u>Do you know why</u>? Even if you have best selling material, had the best cover possible created and hired a world renowned editor to polish your story…..guess what? NOBODY WILL CARE!!

And you can't just create any old platform, grab all the followers and likes as possible and blog away any old stuff. You have to obtain a <u>targeted audience</u>, blog <u>quality content</u> <u>consistently</u>, establish <u>community</u> within your audience and hopefully have loyal people <u>reading</u> your posts and <u>sharing</u>. Do you still want to be a writer?

If so, read on!

<u>Your First Book: Is It all About Ego?</u>

You've had a story idea in the back of your mind. It sits there and stews for months, maybe years. Finally you have the drive to write it. It's one of the most fulfilling things you've ever done. When it's complete, you sit back, interlace your fingers behind your head and think, "Damn, I'm good."

After you edit the first draft and make changes, you give it to your mother, your best friend and your significant other to read through. Mom cries tears of pride, your best friend glows and is so glad she stuck with you and your significant other offers support and guidance, but reads your book with protective trepidation.

All three see nothing wrong with your book and think it's the best thing in the world and it'll fly off the shelves…and they tell you so. Stupidly, you believe them and start researching publishers and agents and formulating your query letter. Is this you?

That was me seven years ago, and I'm not ashamed to admit it, either.

If this is you, you're not alone. However, don't be fooled by your ego and your loved one's biases. If I could turn back the clock, I would do so many things differently.

-<u>Don't submit your first draft</u>, second draft or your third draft to agents or publishers until you've at least had an impartial third party (or two) look at it. I recommend joining Harper Collins's 'Authonomy' (www.authonomy.com) and uploading your book there. Then, after you've made suggested changes, hire a professional editor.

-<u>Please, for the love of god, please don't submit your first</u>, second or third draft to Kindle, Smashwords or any other digital self publishing platform because it's easy and quick and promises huge returns. You're doing nobody a favour, and you'll quickly learn that it's fruitless unless you've taken appropriate steps first.

-<u>Before you even think about submitting</u> your manuscript, develop a platform. It's completely pointless to self publish or attempt to send query letters to publishers or agents without one.

You could have the best material on earth (in your opinion, or in the esteemed opinions of your loved ones), but it isn't just about your book anymore. Don't let your ego stand in the way of doing it right.

<u>Subsidy Publishing-Friend or Foe?</u>

I wrote the following article as I began the daunting task of trying to obtain professional writing experience before I began self publishing my books. This article was submitted to approximately twenty five magazines, rejected by all. It is worth the read to see what perspective I had then, and at the end, I'd like to add my current view if you'll bear with me.

"I have been writing poems since I was around fourteen years old. I started writing short stories when I was in junior high, and now since I've been home for the past five and a half years, I've chosen to write books. It started out as a hobby, but is quickly becoming my strongest passion. I was inspired to write my first book to commemorate what would have been my father's sixtieth birthday. The book is about alcoholism, the disease that took his life at forty one.

"The Message in Dad's Bottle" was compiled from a series of interviews with family members and friends who suffered through alcoholism with their loved one. It took approximately one year to complete, simply because it was difficult to coordinate time to conduct the interviews (I was also at home with two small children at the time).

Finding a publisher for my book was the most difficult process. It took many months of researching publishers within North America. I used the Association of Canadian Publishers website first, and then expanded my search to the US. Most publishers want several specific things, and most items will differ per publisher. It was really hard for me, especially since I hadn't officially published anything. Most publishers are looking for authors who already have a history of published writing. Some would indicate that any published work is only considered professional if you received payment. An interesting catch twenty two.

There was one publisher that did accept my manuscript. After doing some research, I realized that they weren't a traditional publisher. Traditional publishers generally publish, promote and handle all the administration of your book without charging a fee. The publisher that accepted my manuscript is what is commonly referred to as a subsidy publisher. This means that you are charged a fee for their publishing service. Once I was informed of the fee, I regretfully had to turn them down.

My manuscript remained dormant for a number of months. Finally, the publisher that originally accepted my manuscript supplied me with another option. They had a subsidiary company that offered the same service, but instead of covering the charge to keep an inventory of books, they adopted something called "publishing on demand". This means that they only print books as they are ordered, and therefore don't have inventory costs. Thus, the fee would be significantly lower and much more affordable for me.

To be honest, one of the other reasons the book sat for so long was that I was hoping for a traditional publisher to offer me a contract. After doing much more research and sending more manuscript copies out, I discovered that it is extremely difficult for new writers to get published. Most publishers already have a roster of experienced writers with whom they have publishing agreements. Also, publishers only print a specific amount of titles each year and thus the competition is too great for most first time writers such as me.

This book has significant emotional value. I wanted to publish it for my dad's sixtieth birthday. After much contemplation, I decided to go with the "publish on demand" route. I also hoped that once I had a published book, that it would award me the writing experience I required to set the stage for publishing my next book, and perhaps I would have better luck with a traditional publisher then.

The whole publishing process was lengthy, but very enjoyable. Working with my publisher was a memorable experience, and I would recommend them to anyone looking for a subsidy publisher. They did the line editing for a small fee, and they also provided the front cover, which in my opinion is rather striking.

When I received my first copy of the book, it was a truly remarkable experience. The emotion and pride I felt was surely one I will not soon forget. It was certainly a welcome change.

I do not want to discredit my publisher or the parent company because as I stated earlier, it was quite a pleasant experience, and unregretful. Even the costs were justifiable. My publisher performed numerous services and for a reasonable price in my opinion. The issues I encountered occurred after publishing the book, and none of them were the fault of my publisher.

First, the publicity performed to advertise my book was very well put forth, but I soon discovered that my book would likely never be sold in physical bookstores. It would only ever be sold via the internet, through sites such as Amazon.com. Bookstores do not have the room or to put it bluntly, the interest in shelving a book published through a subsidy publisher.

Second, publishing through a subsidy publisher does not constitute "professional writing experience" in the eyes of traditional publishers. This is what I had hoped to obtain. Professional writing experience is viewed as writing a story or an article and having it published in a reputable book or magazine, with or without receiving compensation for it and without having paid a fee.

I suppose this is why they have labeled subsidy publishing as "vanity publishing", as it really only serves to pad the author's ego. It is not a productive method to take if you want to be a professional writer. It will not award you any recognition for having written your book and it is a waste of time to even place your published title on your resume. This, of course, is only in the eyes of traditional publishers.

While I was in the process of researching publishers, I had stumbled upon many websites and forums where would-be authors expressed their outrage for "vanity" publishers. Many of these companies are perceived to have been established solely for the purpose of authors taking the easy road to becoming an accomplished writer. In turn, vanity publishers have also earned themselves a bad reputation for taking advantage of such aspiring authors. Take heed, not all these said publishers are alike. I was very fortunate.

I also tried to apply for a writing grant when I began writing my second book, and was denied. The rejection letter I received from the organization to which I applied stated that "you are not a professional writer" and therefore I would not be entitled to the grant.

Therefore, I will close with this statement: subsidy publishing is the perfect solution for someone who has simply written one book with no future plans for writing. If you are aspiring to be an accomplished author, you must utilize the proper channels. Do not attempt to cut corners; you will ultimately force yourself to start again from scratch."

Fast forward to today, and here I am. Nothing has really changed, except that we are now called "Indie authors" and are viewed entirely different in our own world. We are also striving to gain respect and recognition for our hard work within the publishing world, and are slowly gaining ground in my opinion (and I hope in others' opinions, too).

There is a huge battle between traditional and indie authors as well. Here are a few articles out of probably hundreds circulating.

http://www.derekhaines.ch/vandal/2012/09/self-publishing-authors-are-suspect-and-cheats/

http://www.andreahurst.com/blog/authornomics-interview-with-joanna-penn/

http://shar.es/7KEAC

This one is by far my favourite:

http://www.forbes.com/sites/davidvinjamuri/2012/08/15/publishing-is-broken-were-drowning-in-indie-books-and-thats-a-good-thing/

Set aside the scams, disrespect and freeloaders we have to weed through daily, us indie authors also have to work much harder without pay, and we have to do it blindly. There is no representation for us, because not only do traditional publishers not want to look at us, but neither do agents.

It's really such a shame, because I've spent more hours promoting my work than I've ever spent at a desk, being paid. There has been no income from any of my work, but countless expenses from marketing, promotion and now editing. I continue doing it though, and I'm not giving up. My hope is that when I revisit this article again some day, things will have changed for indie authors, and we'll have broken more ground.

<u>Character Development-Letting Your Baby Go</u>

My manuscript, complete with suggested edits, arrived on my doorstep. When I opened it, I wanted to cry. Many of the painstaking, emotional and well thought out scenes needed to be cut. My idea of character development was completely different, compared to my editor's.
<u>My mistake</u>: swaying too far away from the actual story. The story was lagging and there was not enough action.

<u>My first lesson</u>: character development should occur WHILE the action is taking place.

finger goes to chin Ahhh…..

<u>My second lesson</u>: don't let your ego get in the way of writing a good story. Even if you worked eight hours on a scene; if it isn't part of the meat and potatoes of the story, it needs to go. After all, are you writing the story for yourself?

 Stephen King suggests in his book 'On Writing', that you have to let go of a good chunk of your original manuscript: "eliminate unnecessary words." he says…..Hmmmmmm
As I finished editing my manuscript, and removed almost 21,000 words, my read through was definitely more rewarding. The flow was much better, and the story stayed together and strong throughout.

So remember, just because you sweat and spent hours working on a scene, that doesn't necessarily mean it will fit well. Don't feel like you've wasted time when this happens; think of it more as experience. Not only did you gain from writing a magnificent scene, but you had the wisdom and willpower to remove it. You'll see the rewards, just as I did, when you do your read through. It is worth it. Keep on writing!

<u>Let Your Readers Fall in Love with Your Character, Not Your Plot</u>

In terms of writing a series; this is my opinion.

First, I'll speak from a reader's point of view, then from a writer's.

I've read many series over the years, but my favourite is 'Sue Grafton's A-V mysteries, so I'll use them as my example.

Grafton's main character, Kinsey Millhone, is a relatable, likable, believable person to her reader. Kinsey is a little person in a big world, and essentially on her own, except for her landlord, ninety year old Henry, who the reader also falls in love with. Kinsey is a private investigator, working in a small office. But she kicks ass in every novel and comes out the hero in the end. We all love that, and that's why I've read all A-V in the series; many at least twice.

The most important part about each novel in the Kinsey series, in my opinion, is that the story ties up at the end. Unless your reader has fallen in love with your characters, and they are strong enough characters to hold their own in the next novel, putting a cliff hanger at the end will serve no purpose other than to make the reader feel cheated. It will not initiate the reader to buy the next book. It feels like a money grabber, and a cheap trick.

As a writer, it took the first novel in a series to make me realize this viewpoint. Had I not read the book, I would never have formed this opinion. Therefore, I am thankful that I continue to read as much as I can.

I mean no disrespect to series writers, as there is so much incredible talent in existence. Some series with cliff hangers at the end do have strong enough characters to prompt the reader to want to read the next novel. My belief is that the reader needs more than just a cliff hanger to read on.

I will close with this: it is important as a writer to see things from both viewpoints. We need to write like a reader AND like a writer. There is much to learn from reading, just as from writing.

<u>Tips on How to Write an Honest Book Review</u>

As an indie author, part of your role is to be a reciprocator. Therefore, if you want your book reviewed, you must also review other author's books.

Reviews can sometimes be difficult to write. We don't always know what to say and if we say the wrong thing, we worry about what impact it will have on the author.

Here are some tips I have come up with that help me when I write my reviews.

-Write your review as if the author's mother will be reading it to them. This way you're being honest, but encouraging, not hurtful.

-Write the review immediately after reading the book. Don't begin another book and then go back, the story won't be fresh in your mind.

-Read the book within three weeks. If you give yourself that amount of time and it's not finished, you need to ask yourself
 a) is the book written well enough to keep you interested, and
b) have you devoted enough time to seriously reading the book.

Obviously, if you finish the book before the three weeks is up, you enjoyed it and don't need to address those questions.

-Write the review without bias. If you received the book for free, don't butter up the review because of guilt. You aren't doing the author any favours, and he/she likely gave the book for free in order to get honest reviews to help them improve their story. That works the other way, too, don't give free books and get sour if you receive negative reviews in return.

-Don't give an overly good score on the story unless, in your opinion, it deserves it. We hear far too much about self published authors and the 'halo effect'; or exchanging equally good scores. If it was a good story, score accordingly, if it wasn't, give an appropriate score to reflect your honest level of enjoyment.

-Don't read a book unless it is something you think you would enjoy. If you have a fantasy author chasing you down to read their story and you generally read mystery novels, let them know. If they are willing to accept that you might not enjoy the book and still want you to read it and give them an honest review, then so be it. Don't give them a crappy review though, be upfront in your review and say that it isn't your particular genre of enjoyment. You can still be candid, and likely if it is a well written story, you can still comment on the good points. Also, you might enjoy delving into a new genre, try it!

-Play fair. Remember in order to receive reviews for your book, you must also give them. Conversely, if you have received a review, you should be polite and give one in return. Regardless of your relationship with an author, you should always be honest with your review. Reviews are one of the most important parts of an author's platform, and must be treated as such. This leads to my next point.

-Reviews are tools. Not only does a review help the author improve their story, but they also help promote and sell the book, and build reader trust. If you give a positive review to a story that isn't well written, it dilutes reader trust and doesn't help the author in the long run.

-Reviews are subjective. What one reader thought was a great story could have been bird cage liner to another reader. That is why it is so important to explain what was good and bad about the story, instead of simply providing an opinion. Support your opinion with objective parts about the plot, characters, theme, climax, etc. that you enjoyed. Keep rough notes if necessary to help remind you of these facts.

-Don't think of writing a review like it's homework. We were all assigned book reports back in school, but those were forced, think of writing a review as reflection. I think of mine as journal entries I can come back to when I'm looking for a book to recommend or to re-read.

-Writing reviews can also help you. Take me for example. I review and I'm an author. When I write a review it gives both me and the author exposure. Also, if you write a review for an author who is looking to create relationships with their readers, they will likely try to help you as well. Most of the authors I've reviewed have helped me promote my work and boost my platform, and I've done the same in return.

Always keep in mind that the world of publishing is one where we all need to support one another. When you do something to help out a fellow author, you will likely receive help or support in some way, whether instantly or not. Never underestimate the power of paying it forward. Also, if someone does something like write a review for you, be a good sport and help them out in some way, we are all in this together.

For ideas on how to write a formal book review, I found these websites helpful:

http://www.writing-world.com/freelance/asenjo.shtml

How to Write a Crappy Book

Okay, so you're probably thinking, "What is this girl doing? Who would want to learn how to write a crappy book?" Consider this: we all learned how to write a good book, yes? But we first learned how to write a crappy book. I am no different.

I bet even Bill Gates, when he first began writing software programs, wrote crappy ones. Everything successful begins with a process. Writing is the same. You first learn how to write a crappy book, and then move on to an acceptable one, then a good one and finally a great one.

So........How do we know our books are crappy?

I bet you're thinking "Well, duh, if they don't sell." That's partly right. A book can be the most glorious story ever written, but if it isn't marketed properly, it won't sell. It also won't sell if the author doesn't have an established platform.

You know your book is crappy because:

-It gets no reviews or crappy reviews. Part of getting reviews is giving them. Be sure to give honest reviews or you may not get honest reviews. Please see the previous article for tips on this.

-If you don't get it professionally edited. In my opinion, you need to edit or rewrite your story at least 2-3 times before it is good enough to submit to publishers or to be self published. In my case, my first romance novel was rewritten approximately eight times before I began submitting.

-If it isn't selected for a publishing contract. This is a tricky one. You may have the best story ever written, but if the publishers you have submitted to aren't looking for your type of story, they won't choose it. You need to do your homework on publishers before submitting. Also, each publisher has individual requests, if you don't adhere to their submission guidelines, your manuscript may be tossed into the slush pile.

-If you have an inadequate query letter and/or proposal. This is definitely true in my case. You need professional help from either an editor or a writing coach to sharpen your query letter. That letter is the single most important document aside from a polished manuscript you will send to a publisher/agent.

-If you don't have any training or writing skills. While having training can certainly help you organize your writing and give you good fundamentals, not all successful authors have formal training. Conversely, a trained writer may or may not have the ability to write a good story. It is an art. Story ideas can't be taught. A good story idea most likely can't be made into a good story without coming from the soul of a true writer. Good writing is a gift that few have.

-If you haven't been keeping up with your reading. This means reading for pleasure, to give reviews, and to learn more about writing/building your platform. You can't do it alone, and if you try, you'll be sure to write a crappy book. Reading is so important in order to write well.

-If you haven't been engaging with other authors. Successful authors have established a solid platform and most will gladly share tips on how to build one. That's part of the beauty of being a writer; in order to become successful you will have helped others along the way. You must give in order to receive. Paying it forward is very important when you're a writer.

Once you've written a few crappy books, you'll learn what it's like to begin writing good ones. In other words, you'll get practice. Some self published authors go about it backwards by writing a book, publishing it without getting it edited, and then try to build their platform by marketing the heck out of it. I'm not ashamed to admit that that's exactly how I did it. Twice. Don't make that same mistake. Your books will not sell and you'll have to start from scratch as I've been doing.

Follow all these steps and learn more valuable steps. Share your knowledge. Read, read and then read some more. Never give up. Never let others give up. Think positive and support others in doing so. Remember: Rome wasn't built in a day. No good books were ever written in a day either. I bet a few crappy ones were ☺

10 Common Mistakes Made in Your First Draft

After having my second romance novel professionally edited, I thought it would be neat to keep the original draft and compare the two to see what common mistakes were made. I thought by sharing them, it might help those currently working on a manuscript avoid these mistakes or look out for them when editing.

-Incorrect placement of quotation marks.

My quotation marks were put before the period in most of my dialogue. They actually belong after. Your sentence needs to end before the quotation mark.

Wrong: "Oh, honey, it's not your fault".

Right: "Oh, honey, it's not your fault."

-Capitalizing 'he said' or she said' at the end of dialogue. This is self explanatory, but I'll give an example.

Wrong: "Oh, honey, it's not your fault." She said.

Right: "Oh, honey, it's not your fault." She said.

-Using a period instead of a comma within the dialogue. This gets tricky. If the dialogue is complete and the thought has ended, then you would use a period, but my common mistake was to use a period in each case.

Wrong: "Good evening, Sarah's." she greeted cheerfully. "It's me." I said, trying to stifle a sniffle.

Right: "Good evening, Sarah's," she greeted cheerfully. "It's me," I said, trying to stifle a sniffle.

-The semi-colon vs. period vs. comma argument. This was probably my most common mistake. When I should have used a period, I used a semi-colon, and where I should have used a period, I used a comma.

Wrong:

"He sounded weird and said I better come home; that he wasn't feeling well."

Right:

"He sounded weird and said I better come home, that he wasn't feeling well."

Wrong:

"I've got a meeting at school today. Preparation for September; it's only five weeks away you know."

Right:

"I've got a meeting at school today. Preparation for September. It's only five weeks away you know."

Wrong:

"It's delicious…the guys will like it too, did you make lots?"

Right:

"It's delicious….the guys will like it too. Did you make lots?"

-Whether to use the comma or period before dialogue. I always used the period or nothing where I should have used the comma.
Wrong:

I asked the inevitable question "Can I see him?"

Right:

I asked the inevitable question, "Can I see him?"

-To break up a sentence with a comma or period or not. I had trouble deciding on the flow of some sentences, so I mostly threw in a comma for good measure. Wrong. My best advice is to read the sentence out loud. If you have to take a breath to finish the sentence, it likely needs a comma (or period).

Wrong:

I knew Jennifer couldn't handle this; she had just broken up with her first boyfriend, so I thought it best to wait.

Right:

I knew Jennifer couldn't handle this, she had just broken up with her first boyfriend, so I thought it best to wait.

-Starting a new paragraph when needed. I would continue dialogue in the same paragraph when I should have begun a new one.

Wrong:

My eyes followed Mark as he came closer to me, looking at me suspiciously. He played along, "Really? A luscious meal huh…what's this about good fortune? I didn't play the lotto today." I shook my head, "No, it said MY good fortune." He nodded and his eyebrows rose. "Yeah, but your good fortune is HALF mine, right?"

Right:

My eyes followed Mark as he came closer to me, looking at me suspiciously.

He played along, "Really? A luscious meal huh….what's this about good fortune? I didn't play the lotto today."

I shook my head, "No, I said MY good fortune."

He nodded and his eyebrows rose, "Yeah, but your good fortune is HALF mine, right?"

-Repetitiveness. For some reason I liked saying 'winked' a lot after dialogue, or 'she looked at him like he had two heads', or the worst ones were constant crying or referring to people being late: 'he texted her to say he would be late', or she would be late for dinner again tonight. When you see a theme being repeated, switch it up or delete it.

-Improper use of description. For example, after dialogue 'she returned', or 'she offered', when simply 'she said' would have sufficed.

-Using too many words. This is a tough one when it's your first draft, because we tend to let the words flow out (which we should when it's our first draft, as that's the best way to get your ideas out). Just remember to go back and cut the fat.

Wrong: We lay in bed together the whole night, making love for many hours, so glad to be united forever.

Right: We lay in bed the whole night, making love for many hours. (the scene would have already eluded to a wedding, so the last piece would have been repetitive)

Hopefully you found these tips helpful. My best advice is to get your manuscript professionally edited. It is imperative in my opinion in order to polish and make your story flow well and clearly. The difference between my first and last draft is astounding. Just cutting the fat alone eliminated 25k words.

A good editor will critique your work and tell you what parts don't work and why. They'll also tell you if something is missing. The writer often can't see that. Because we wrote it, we know what certain scenes imply, but we may not realize it isn't obvious to the reader.

Don't ever feel like you did an inadequate job if you get your manuscript back and there are tons of edits to be done. Editing, like writing, is a process. It may look like your editor thinks your story is terrible based on the stuff he/she wants removed, but that isn't true. If I can survive having 25, 000 words eliminated from mine and still live to tell about it, you can too.

Do You Like Weak Blogs or Strong Blogs?

That's a pretty dumb question, isn't it? It would seem obvious, but to some it's not. If you're an indie writer, I'll bet my life you're also a blogger. If you're not.....well......get on it! If you are a blogger and you haven't joined Triberr (www.triberr.com), I highly recommend that you do.

I've seen some wonderfully informative and inspirational blogs since joining Triberr. I'm no expert myself; learning as I go is part of the experience.

But one thing I've learned is that focus is important. I don't mean focus on one topic and go at it like crazy. Personally, I have four separate blog topics. You need lots of subject matter if you're going to offer posts at least three times a week, which is what I strive for.

From a reader's perspective, most posts are absolutely spot on, but recently I've seen a few that read like the writer is drawing at straws. I understand that blogging is the way to get traffic to your website, and for some, a way to make money.

But consider this: if you're posting to draw attention to your site to sell books, you may need to tighten up your work. Your readers are reading your posts as a representation of your writing skills and imagination. If you're writing weak articles, readers may construe that to mean that you have weak writing skills.

My method is this, (and again, I'm not saying I'm an expert) I keep a diary, both a physical and a digital one (my cell phone). When an idea pops into my head, (through reading, writing, networking or life in general) I write it down with as much detail as I can. Then I write on my laptop as immediately as possible. Even if it's only a paragraph. Then I save it and come back to it later when I have more to add. More on this later.

I'm lucky in that I began to journal years ago. My book Just When I Needed to Laugh was created by simple daily journal entries of all the funny and cute things my kids said. It turned into a book, and now I blog that book. There's tons of material.

If you can journal your ideas, you'll have tons of material to work with, too. Hopefully that material will lend itself to a strong blog, and will compliment your writing style.
In my opinion, when bloggers draw at straws, it means that they are exhausting themselves. When this happens (and it's happened to me, too), you need to step back and focus on something else for a day or two.

I think posting every day is too much, unless you have strong material. It should be about quality, not quantity. If you're not providing quality material, readers will lose interest and you may not get the reach you previously enjoyed. Remember: when readers share your material, it also effects their reputation. If you aren't providing strong posts, you risk losing shares.

If you have less shares or website traffic for one day, does it really make that big of a difference if it means you'll offer a stronger post the next day? You may even get more reach by waiting. After all, good things come to those who wait.

The other important thing when you're a blogger is editing. While most of the material I've seen is perfect, I'm also seeing blogs that should have had an additional proof read before being posted. What I do is read it out loud to myself several times. Then I read it to my husband (who is very meticulous and critical), and make necessary changes.

Again, if you're a writer and you're blogging unedited material, it doesn't bode well for your writing style.

I'm not saying that everything has to be perfect. I just updated the front page of my website, and noticed I spelled the word children 'chilren'. I'm not perfect, either. But we should try to be as perfect as possible when we're writing for public viewing.

If You Wouldn't Read it to Your Mother, Would You Read it Yourself?

Do Love Scenes Make or Break a Book's Chances of Being Read?

When my first romance novel was published, I noticed some people shied away from it simply because it has an adult filter on it.

I've read my share of romance novels, even non-romance novels with some pretty hefty love scenes in them, and I was never deterred from reading through to the last page. Am I the only one who feels this way?

For some, it's just taste. If a book contains graphic sex not relevant to the story, then I can understand why they wouldn't be interested in reading an inconsistent story line. But if the love scenes are part of the character's development, why wouldn't they appreciate that as part of the plot?

In my first romance novel, the first love scene is slightly more graphic, but the second is sweet and warm and in keeping with the romance evolving in the main character's life. The act of love making is important in love stories, in my opinion, just as it is in life. After all, as a reader aren't we supposed to be there in the story? Aren't we supposed to feel, see and experience what our characters are experiencing? Therefore as a writer, isn't it my job to illustrate every element for my readers?

Creating deeply emotional and physical scenes is a craft, and I think if you remove the love making, you take away from the whole picture. So why deprive readers of that experience?

My point is that it is wrong to assume that because a book is listed as 18+, that it contains explicit sex scenes that if you don't subscribe to Penthouse, you won't enjoy. Keep an open mind and enjoy a story for what it is.

How many mothers out there would enjoy a good, wholesome love scene anyway? My mother read my book and loved it. Okay, she was biased, but still!

15 Tips for the First Day of Your KDP Select FREE Promotion

-Make sure your book is polished (properly edited, catchy title, etc.)

-Create your own cover or hire a great cover designer (or a free service like www.myecovermaker.com)

-Give your book a great hook/pitch-both short and long (you will need a short one for Twitter and a long one for all your book promoting social media sites)

-Publish it on Amazon.com and Kindle Direct Publishing (make sure it isn't available on any other digital platform ie. Smashwords)

-Ask your friends, Twitter followers, etc. to like your book and give it a quick review once it's on the site. (give out copies to friends before publication date). Even one or two reviews and likes will look better than none. (You can even swap some likes with your Twitter friends).

-Set your book up on Kindle for the promotional free 5 days. (go to your bookshelf, select your book, click on 'actions', then 'manage promotions', and enter the applicable information).

Note: you can use all 5 free days at once, or you can break them up. I used all 5 because I've noticed my blogs sometimes take that long to circulate throughout my platform. Make sure you choose days where your schedule isn't too busy as you'll need to keep on top of your progress, etc.

-Put your book information on the home page of your website and be sure to add your promotion dates and a link to where they can get your book for free. Be sure to make it stand out; use lots of colours, italics, large text, etc.

-Create a blog with your book's title named first. Put your long pitch and a compelling excerpt from your book in your blog, along with the link to get it for free, and don't forget to tell them the days that it will be free.

-Post your blog to all your social media outlets (although I highly
recommend Triberr, Google+, LinkedIn, Twitter, Facebook (your fan page as well as your personal page), Pinterest and any other site you're using.

-Post your blog on all your groups, communities, book clubs, etc. (I highly recommend Google+ communities, LinkedIn groups, Goodreads, etc.)

Note: If you're on Goodreads, make sure your Author page is set up to receive your blog's RSS feed. Then your blog introducing your book's promotion will automatically upload on to Goodreads. Make sure you've also set up your Author page for a free giveaway of your physical book, this can give you double the exposure since your Goodreads friends may be navigating to your site to enter into the contest.

-Get your book on as many Free e-book promotion sites as possible. This may take some strategic planning ahead of time, since most sites have a backlog of books to feature for free. Try as many as you can, one or two is better than none.

The sites I recommend are:

Ereader News Today (ENT) Free Book
Submissions http://www.ereadernewstoday.com
Free Kindle Books and
Tips http://www.fkbooksandtips.com
Pixel of Ink Free & Bargain Kindle
Books http://www.pixelofink.com (Note: you can also list
your book here when it's not free; if you're just offering a
discount)
Author Marketing
Club http://www.authormarketingclub.com

-Make sure you have completed your KDP (Kindle Direct
Publishing) profile on Author Central. This will help readers
see who you are, what work you've done, etc.

-Do regular tweet updates, letting people know how well your
book is doing; it acts as an incentive and makes it less
redundant as you're constantly reminding them to take
advantage of the promotion while it lasts. To access your
sales stats, go on to your KDP main page and select 'reports',
then select 'Month to Date Sales' and look at the column 'Free-
Units Promo' to see where you're at.

-Post your blog the first 2 days of your promotion, adding a
line something like 'in the first __ hours, my book sold ___, get
yours free!' On the third day, change your line to 'Just 2 days
left to get ___for free! Don't Miss Out!' As long as you're
reminding your audience that there's still time.

-Be sure to thank, retweet and respond to any and all
comments, mentions, or anything that someone says about
your book during your promotional time, and any time after
that, really. Maintaining engagement with your audience will
give you a better chance at having a larger fan base.

With the sale of my first 2 books, I did none of these things. The only thing I did was post the link to where my book could be found on my personal Facebook page, and I did a PR spread. I sold none, well, my second book I actually sold 5 but that was from my book signings.

The lesson learned was that I needed to do much more work developing my platform BEFORE trying to sell my books (which is why step#9 will be pointless if you haven't already established your platform on all those sites). After my second book launched, I had just finished my third, and at that time I began building my platform incessantly.
Countless hours each day were spent researching, registering for other sites, creating blogs, reading hundreds of blogs from more successful authors, learning what they did right.

5 More Tips to Make the Best out of Your KDP Select FREE Promotion Days

Day 2 of my KDP Select promotional days, I admit, was slow. But I did 5 simple things to speed things up:

-Utilize Hootsuite and tweet every 30 minutes with your link.
-Retweet as others make mention of your blogs and tweets (it's amazing how many people will retweet when you've got a promotion going on)

-Jump on another author's promotional band wagon (I mean as many as you can). When another author retweets or mentions your promotional stuff, jump on their profile and pick up the first tweet making mention of their promotion or just their work. I found my twitter mentions basically doubled after doing this.

-Thank people who help you with your promotion. Even if they don't have a promotion in the works, and they simply help you by retweeting out of the kindness of their hearts, don't forget about them.

-Don't forget to hop on all your forums, communities, etc. and respond to all mentions or comments. Very important.

(tip: I had a few negative comments during my promotional period. I responded only to the positive ones.)

I'd like to take this opportunity to mention some people who really helped me during my promotion.

-John Dolan (@JohnDolanAuthor) If you don't follow John yet, do yourself a favour. He actually autotweeted my promotion through his platform the entire 5 days. I can't thank him enough. He's been a huge supporter of mine since we first connected. John is also a very talented writer, and the author of a book I read personally 'Everyone Burns'
http://johndolanwriter.blogspot.com/search/label/Home

In no particular order, these people were the most helpful to me:

-Garry Pritchard (@GarryPritchard)
-Orchard Book Club (@OrchardBookClub)
-Mel (2g2lmel) author of Me, My World and I.
-Malla Duncan (@MallaDuncan)
-Ron Dahle (@chrningcauldron) The Churning Cauldron
http://www.churningcauldron.com
-Peggy Edelheit (@samanthajamison) author of The Puzzle, Without any Warning to name a few
http://samanthajamison.com

-Michael J. McCann (@MichaelJMcCann1) author of the
Donoghue and Stainer Crime Novel
Series www.mjmccann.com
-Josef Kotzbauer
(@Dessousandmore) http://www.dessous-for-
dreaming.de/
-Daniel Kemp (@danielkemp6) author of The Desolate
Garden http://www-thedesolategarden-com.co.uk/
-KRRowe (@KRRowe) author of Amber and
Blue http://t.co/DkrK56kF
-Marlin Williams (@Marlin2002)

There were so many more, but too many to list.
This is merely a 'this is what I did, and this was the result'. I
began my first day with 450 downloads and by the end of day
4, I was at 939 downloads. I know for some this is peanuts,
but for me, considering this was my debut novel, I'd say it
wasn't bad at all.

My Kindle FREE Promotion is Over.....Now What?

I asked myself the same question. Even after having 1580
downloads of my first romance novel, I was on a high that
quickly plummeted as sales netted zero the minute the
promotion ended.

So, what do you do? Keep promoting! Here's a list of the
things I did:

-Set up Hootsuite to tweet every 30 or 60 minutes. Experiment
with tweets and see if they net you sales. Change them up!
Don't use the same tweets over and over again. Save some in
drafts and alternate.

-Keep blogging! Blog, blog, blog and keep your website
as active and current as possible.

-Jump on another person's promo wagon. Very important. When someone retweets your promo tweets, retweet them back! Be polite and it will net you huge retweets. I got so many, I almost couldn't keep up.

-Utilize sites that offer promotion. Here are some that I used:

-AskDavid.com

This was by far the best site. All I had to do was place a link to their site on my website and my ad got pushed to the top and completed immediately. Here's the link:
http://askdavid.com

-Goodreads.com

I've been on Goodreads a long time, and so far the returns have been okay. You can have contests to win free books, buy ad space, or start/join a forum and other author tools are also available. The returns aren't bad, but so far minimal sales. That's just my own experience, yours could be different.

Here's the link:

http://www.goodreads.com
-MyKindleMojo.com

If you donate to this site, you are automatically placed on their recommended reads, however, if you don't you can still be there, it just takes longer. The book profiles are a little difficult to navigate, but if you provide the link to your audience it should be easy enough:

http://www.kindlemojo.com

-BookTalk.org

I found this site to be very useful if you purchase ad space. Fortunately at the time they had a special and I took advantage. It was just $120.00 for 3 months on a 'Featured Authors' page, and then a permanent ad on their book site. Here is the link:

http://www.booktalk.org

-LibraryThing.com

This site reminds me very much of Goodreads. You create a profile both as a reader and an author, add your authored books and the books you're reading or have read and any reviews. The site I found to be a little fussy. You have to navigate through many radio buttons and screens to get where you want to be.

-Absolute Write Water Cooler.com

Set up in an old school way, but offers many forums you can join or just post a reply. I couldn't find one applicable to what I wanted, so I created my own.

Should You Help Promote a Book You Haven't Read?

Here's a thought: Is it the same thing as retweeting a blog post you haven't read? Hmmmmm…….

I suppose reading a blog and reading an entire book are two completely different things. But do either hurt your reputation if you promote them without having read them?

I think when you retweet a blog you haven't read, and it's not a great post, it *can* impact your reputation. This is especially true if the post is offensive or badly written. Hence, you should take the time to at least *skim through blog content.* (see my next article 'Do You Actually Read Other People's Blog Posts' for my thoughts on this).

Here are some of my points:

-Assuming your audience has read the same book, or seen the promotional material and thinks the book looks enjoyable/unenjoyable or likes the author/doesn't like the author, does it have any effect on your audience?

-What if you *have* read the book and promote it, does it make a difference to your audience?

-How does this affect your non-writing audience? (or some of your non-target audience members).

-Does this have any effect on your audience members from different genres?

-What about promoting books that support controversial topics?

-Is it all just a matter of opinion? Or do most people simply ignore posts that don't relate to or interest them?

My thought is that we should read through blog posts before promoting them, simply because of the exposure. It is much easier to read through a post and forward it than to read an entire book and promote it. People are also more inclined to read blog posts than to read book reviews.

I'll conclude by saying that my opinion is it's okay to promote a book that you haven't read. You can read it later (and you can make that public by placing it on your to-read shelf on Goodreads.com).

It would be very sad if it wasn't acceptable to promote a book you haven't read because it's so easy to do! It also helps the author, and being an author myself, I find the easiest way to promote my work is to jump on someone else's promotional band wagon.

Are You Actually Reading Other People's Blog Posts?

We're all pressed for time. We all want to keep our social media content flowing.

One question: do you retweet or approve a blog post before actually reading it?
I admit…I'm guilty.

Problem: you could be posting not-so-great content without actually knowing it.

See 'The Top Ten reasons I Never Visit Your Blog Anymore' by @amberrisme, here's the link:

http://rantitude.com/top-10-reasons-i-never-visit-your-blog-anymore

The blog touches on items such as weak content, poor site setup, profanity, etc. When you see an interesting post title and think 'well, the title is good, the content must be, too', you could be posting something unfavourable to your audience, the ones who actually read your posts, and you could lose valuable members of your platform.

My suggestion: Read blogs before retweeting or mentioning them!
While you're at it, if you're going to take the time to read a good post, leave a comment.
This helps you and the author of the post. How?

You're helping them build their community AND YOUR OWN in that their community will see YOU and hopefully link to your site.

Also, if the post is really good, you'll have learned something from it. Isn't that really what it's all about? Engagement.

And hey, the comment you leave may initiate conversation, especially if the moderator graciously leads your comment back to your blog. This once again comes down to quality vs. quantity.

Tip: Make sure you have a plugin installed on your blog so that your audience can leave a plug for themselves with their website and/or blog link. This acts as an incentive for them. When I installed LiveFyre, I noticed my comments increased almost immediately. I've also seen Commentluv and a few others. If you use Wordpress for your site, simply go to your dashboard, click on plugins, and do a search. It's really easy.

What is Your Literary Lifeline?

It's kind of funny actually. Some people think I'm a textaholic, when in fact I'm not. My Blackberry is essentially my literary lifeline. Without it, I'd be struck with an idea and nowhere to record it for safekeeping.

Ideas strike me at very odd times, and if you're like me, your cell phone is basically an appendage of your hip. I use it for everything. I even keep alarms so I know when it's time to move on to another task.

I think the number one reason why some bloggers have, shall we say, 'blah blogs', is because they've run out of ideas. This doesn't mean that their creative energy has run dry, just that they had a creative streak and didn't take advantage.

Whether that means they didn't run to their computer and type away or they didn't take note, either way if you don't record your ideas when they're unleashed, how will you ever remember them?

Here's a breakdown of the lists that I maintain in my Blackberry:

-Blog ideas (notes or rough drafts)
-Book (storyline) ideas
-Title ideas (for books or blogs)
-Challenging questions to prompt me to remember things exactly as they were in my mind.
-Things to do
-Notes/excerpts for my book/blog
-Ideas for writing style (usually from reading other books)
-Books to read
-Blog titles/bloggers to read

Hubby even sometimes throws ideas for stuff my way, and I immediately take note. Some of my best blog ideas have come from him. Ideas even creep up sometimes when I'm talking on the phone or when I have company.

My kids say the funniest things and if I don't immediately record them, they're lost forever. If you always have your phone handy, why not use it? You never know if you'll ever get that idea back. What have you got to lose?

To Join KDP Select or Not....That is the Question

I self published my first romance novel back in early December 2012, and I submitted it to the KDP Select program immediately thereafter.

The free promotion period I chose was for one week in mid-December. What a rush that was! Holy cow! My blog posted to all my communities, groups, etc. and when the end of the promotional period was over, I had over 1600 downloads......Hooray!!!

......or not.

After being on a major high; feeling loved and popular and almost certain my hard work was finally going to pay off...I thought 'Oh boy! Think of all the reviews I'm going to get! Things are really going to take off for me!! Woooohooooo!'.....yeah, not so much.

Not only did I get minimal sales after my promotion ended, but I got only two reviews. Not that I'm complaining or didn't appreciate what I received, because none of these people had to download, read *or* review my book. I just want to convey the message that there are no guarantees. Don't get your hopes up.

What's worse is that while everyone else was posting huge discounts, especially after Christmas, I was stuck in KDP Select prison. Then, to top it off, people were asking me if my book was available for Kobo and other digital formats....um....no, not until March 10.

I had actually considered removing my book from KDP Select so I could re-publish it on Smashwords with my other books and give it out at a nice discount. But after reading the fine print (and kicking myself for not reading it BEFORE signing), I noticed that you still are bound to KDP Select for the three month period even IF you remove your book from it.

You're still not allowed to put your book on any other digital platform until the three month period ends.
Be informed, make calculated decisions, but above all remember that there are no guarantees. I hope your KDP Select experience serves you well, if you do decide to join.

The Writer/Reader-A Jekyll and Hyde Character

I wondered for days why people wouldn't want to buy a story that was only 99 cents. Even when you go to the Dollar Store and buy an item that lasts only 5 minutes, you still don't feel cheated, so why would someone hesitate to buy a 99 cent book? It's not the money...is it the time?

Picture this. You're an avid reader. You've had a long week at work and you just can't wait to sit down to a chilled glass of wine and a good book. Friday night approaches and you get into your jammies, get the kids to bed and snuggle on your couch with your book in hand. You start reading and the book is nothing like what you expected.

The disappointment ruins your evening, puts you in a bad mood and sours your entire weekend. You never look that author up again.

My opinion is this is why avid readers like to get books for free when they're trying out a new author. It's that small difference between paying for something and not that's the deal breaker. If they didn't pay a cent and the book sucked, they just move on.

Months ago I got a book for free. Loved the beginning, but the middle and end were predictable, juvenile and then the author put a cliff hanger at the end to try to entice the reader to actually buy the next book to see what happens next in the story. That author immediately lost a spot on my bookshelf. The fact that I didn't pay for the book made it slightly better, but the cheated feeling soured my impression of the author indefinitely.

Isn't it funny how that happened? Would I give the author a second chance? Absolutely not. If the book is a turn off, I move on to the next author. My time means way more to me than that.

But in thinking about this, something occurred to me. We have to remember that authors write different storylines, topics and some even different genres (that's me), so keeping an open mind is essential when continuing to read from an author's backlist. If I were a reader reading from my own backlist, I'd be sunk.

What if Readers Don't Use the 'Look Inside' Feature?

I was responding to a reader who commented on the previous article about reading 99 cent books, when I realized something may be terribly wrong.

The comment was regarding the 'Look Inside' feature on Amazon.com. Most people I assume use it when making book buying decisions; if they like the supplied excerpt they buy, if not then they move on.
It occurred to me that perhaps our 'freebie hoarders' just download our free books during our KDPS promotion, only to delete them later if they don't like them. The reader suggested that this may be happening so Kindle owners can simply fill their e-reader.

Pause.....sorry, I just fainted.

How would this impact our overall sales outlook?

Well, this would be really really BAD! It would give us a false sense of success after our promotion....a REALLY false sense. Hello? Inflated Egos Anonymous? Yes, I need help!

Let's face it. When we put our books on their Kindle free promotion, it's in hopes that at least some of the readers will read, enjoy, like, rate and if we're really lucky, review our book.

But this only works if they actually intend to read it. Be mindful of this during your next promotion.

Book Sales Hit a Slump?

In conversation with other, more seasoned authors, they shared a few tips with me on how they got their books out of their sales slump. I've done them all.

Here's a list:

-Freshen up your book cover. This is by far the one that will have the most impact.
I used the free program myecovermaker.com

Tip: be sure to view the tutorial-very helpful.

I also use the picture database Inmagine.com, which is a source for both paid and royalty free photos.

Tip: when searching for pictures, be sure to click on 'royalty free' and be sure to select pictures with the 'RF' logo under the image.

With a little practice creating covers, you'd be amazed at the end product. Or you can always hire a professional cover designer.

-Add top reviewer's quotes on the first page of your book.

Hopefully you've been able to get some reviews from your readers. What I recommend using are those from book clubs and other authors. Be sure to mention the reviewer's name and the name of their book (or the name of the club they're affiliated with) under
the quote.
-Add top reviewer's quotes on the home page of your website.

Do the same thing as in the previous step, but also use the quote feature (the button with the quotation marks) if you use Wordpress, to make your quotes stand out.

-Use Hootsuite to add interesting quotes from your book to your tweets.

For tips on this, please see the next article 'How to Tweet Your Book-5 Easy Steps'

-Use Facebook Ads (sponsored stories).

I get approximately 50% more visits to my website when I post blogs under sponsored stories. This works well when you post about writing and include links to your book.

-Blog more often. See above tip.

-Freshen up your webpage (add your book covers to your site if you haven't already). If you use Wordpress, you can use the 'Jetpack' image feature to add your books to your site. If your theme doesn't support this, you can switch to the paid Socrates theme (or choose a different unpaid theme). Here's hoping if you are in a sales slump, that these tips will help.

How to Tweet Your Book-5 Easy Steps

We all know how to TWEET, but do we all know how to TWEET A BOOK? It sounds pretty simple, but I have a few little tricks to share.

-Select excerpts or favorite lines in your book, copy and paste them into a Word document.

What I also recommend is actually going through your book in chunks, and choosing specific pieces that you think are catchy (without having to read the before part to understand), that will draw your reader's attention.

The first time I did this, I chose about ten. Save them all in a Word document and then open up your Hootsuite account. (www.hootsuite.com). If you don't have one, it's really easy to set up, and to start, you only need to set up Hootsuite for Twitter, not for any of the other social media sites.

-Click on 'compose message', select your Twitter profile to your right (to activate the character counter), and begin typing in your first excerpt. You'll have to play around and edit your excerpt to fit into the allowable number of characters. This is why I only chose ten to start.

-Cut and paste the link to Amazon.com or wherever your book is available into the 'add a link' field and click on 'shrink'. You can even do this before you add your excerpt since the link will take up characters and you'll have to re-edit afterwards.

-Click on the save button (looks like a floppy disc). This will save your excerpt including your link and Twitter profile into your drafts.

-Click on the calendar to schedule your tweet. Continue doing this with all your excerpts until you have a nice collection to get started.

Once you have your ten excerpts saved in drafts, all you have to do is click on the arrow beside the save button to retrieve them. You can schedule them as often as you like (I did mine every half hour). I also recommend tweeting your short pitch and links to any promotional websites your book can be found on as well.

Tip: Don't forget to schedule Tweets around the clock. There are people all over the world in different time zones who may catch your tweets!

I found that once I had a nice pattern of tweets, I also received a nice influx of retweets from my audience. To gain return on those, be sure to return the favor and retweet back. Jumping on another author's promotional band wagon is the best way to receive more retweets and support.

Tip: You can also use Hootsuite to post your book excerpts into other social media sites, you don't have to just use Twitter!

Places to Market Your Book for Free or Minimum Cost

You've hit a slump in book sales and don't know where to go. Is this you? I feel your pain....I did a quick Google search and came up with a few goodies that I'll share with you.

-Kobo (www.kobobooks.com)

Make sure your book isn't still on KDPS when you submit it to Kobo, but essentially it's a free service that enables your book to be distributed on their database, which includes Chapters/Indigo and W.H. Smith to name a couple. You need to have your book in epub format with an eISBN to submit.

-Indie Bound (www.indiebound.org)

I was surprised to find that two out of my three published books were already on this site. I just needed to update my cover for my first romance novel. There isn't an actual link to add books to this site, but if you send them a general email they send you a response with the appropriate email addresses and instructions as to how to add your book(s) and again, it's free.

This site also offers an affiliate program (just like Amazon) so it's worth looking into if you have ad space on your site.

-Just Romantic Suspense (http://justromanticsuspense.com)

This is paid advertising, but it only costs $15.00 a month. It's great if you want a target audience looking at your work. Their lead time is only a week to get your ad on their site and their site looks very professional, complete with rotating advertisements for your book. I was impressed personally.

-We Really Dig Romance Novels (www.wereallydig.com/romancenovels/index.html) Although the site title is a little lame, again, it's free advertising. They even review your book if you send them an electronic copy.

-Romance Junkies (www.romancejunkies.com)

Again, a cheesy title, but if you email them a copy of your book, they review it and place it on their site for free. Be sure to use the drop down menu and select 'author services' for info.

Tip: If you haven't already done so, try Facebook Ads. What I suggest is to open up at least two ads and use different test markets. Once they're approved, come back in a day or two and check out the reports. See which one has had more clicks and check it against your sales. Even if you've originally placed your ad at a high bid, you can always pause or delete it if it isn't worthwhile.

How Important are Reviews and Likes Anyway?

Have you ever wondered what would happen if book marketing platforms like Amazon didn't have the 'Like' or 'Review' features?

When you're a new author, these features are pretty scary and you almost wish they weren't there. You look at other established authors who have hundreds of likes (well, maybe not that many) and so many reviews that you can't even get through them all and think......how on earth am I going to get those?

So you ask your friends and family and beg people on your fan site (if you have one) to like your book on Amazon and offer contests for people to read and review your book. That's exactly what I did. Some of it worked, but then I got to thinking: how is this legitimate? Sure it looks good, but I thought it was a little transparent, so I stopped.

If you're going to go after reviews, you need to get them from legitimate reviewers: other authors, book clubs and unbiased readers.

Think about it. When you go to purchase a book (one that isn't well known) and see reviews that are questionable (ie. one-liners, "oh, this book is wonderful and I couldn't put it down", positive comments with no reference to the story and *why* the book was so wonderful), would you buy it?

You must also remember that your potential readers aren't just going to look at your reviews as criteria for purchasing your book. Your blurb, cover and first chapter must be extremely appealing. Some of the feedback I've received from past posts point to the reviews being less important; the cover, blurb and first chapter are paramount in deciding whether or not to buy the book.

My point is this: Don't worry so much about your reviews. Before publishing your book, make sure you've had at least a few unbiased people (beta readers) read it and review it. But more importantly, make sure you give your cover, blurb and first chapter (and don't forget about the rest of the book) everything you've got. If those three things are your absolute best work; reviews, likes and hopefully sales will come.

How to Come up with Book Ideas

I'm not great at book marketing; I'll admit that. Nor am I great with platform building; I'm learning as I go. But I will tell you that I *definitely* know how to come up with good book ideas. Here's how:

-Read, read, read, read, read…..did I mention read?

The testament "if you want to read a book that hasn't been written yet, you must write it" is so true. Most of my book ideas have come from this sentiment.

Some of my favourite authors are Sue Grafton, John Grisham, Nicholas Sparks, Philippa Gregory, E.L. James and Andrew Morton. By reading all these author's books, I've derived my favourite storylines and what I feel would make a great story.

-Take Notes

Never EVER leave your house without some way of taking notes. Ideas will pop into your head out of the blue. If you have no way of taking note, how will you remember them? The smallest idea could turn into the largest, best idea for a story.

When I was beginning to write my first book, I began taking notes of all the funny things my kids said and did. This gave birth to my second (unpublished) book.

-Get a good night's sleep

So many of my story ideas pop into my head as I'm waking in the morning; that is, if I'm well rested. The idea for my first romance novel came to me after finishing Nicholas Sparks' 'A Walk to Remember'. The next morning, I literally wrote the guts for that novel. The same thing happened when I wrote the sequel to my second romance novel; I was in the process of editing and one morning it just popped into my head; I began writing that same day.

-Write…dammit!

If you've taken notes, read a lot and are sleeping well, you have the foundation for good writing. The next step is to sit down and write. You cannot begin or finish a book until you've begun writing and that's sometimes the scariest part.

When I began writing my second romance novel, it started with a shadow of an idea. I had no idea where the story would take me. It was almost like the book was being born with each scene. Before I knew it I had chapters and chapters of action and dialogue….and I knew how it would end!

-Self Confidence

Many writers I've noticed call themselves 'aspiring writers'. Why? If you're a writer, you're a writer. There is no grey area. Don't think that because you're not Stephen King or Nicholas Sparks that you can't be a writer. If you have the drive to do it, the tools are there.

I don't have a degree in writing or any formal training aside from my college diploma. But I've successfully written six books. If you have poor grammar or spelling, that's what your editors are there for. It's the marketing and promoting that's the hard part; I'm still learning about that. But the point is if you want to write, do it. *Just do it right.*

-Be Serious

If you've written a book and put every ounce of effort and energy into it; bled your heart and soul into it with every spare moment you've had for months.....please be serious. Don't let your ego take over. Don't run out and self publish through Amazon or any other digital platform without taking the appropriate steps. Do get it professionally edited, do hire a professional cover designer, do establish a platform and last, do get it beta read. Please don't be the 'hey, I'll sell it and be a millionaire' type. There are too many of those out there...and frankly, they're giving us indie authors a bad name.

-Write What's in Your Heart

Some blogs I've read over the past year have said to pay attention to market trends for books. Know your audience and be sure to write what will sell. I find that to be troublesome personally. *How can you write what's trendy?* Believe me, I've tried. I once wrote a short erotica story, having read that erotica was hugely popular. The writing was hot and steamy, but the storyline was terrible! Maybe I'm just not an erotica writer? Perhaps. But I think it's more to do with the fact that I *wasn't writing from my heart.* Writing is an art...cliché, I know. But it's true. Be a leader, not a follower, and write what comes naturally to you. You can't put your best effort into it if your heart isn't there.

-Listen, live, laugh and be positive.

Have you met any grumpy writers lately? I didn't think
so. The world of writing is a place where we all join together
and help one another. You will never make it as a
writer unless it makes you happy. You have to take the good
with the bad; I'll be honest, *writing your book is only half the
battle*, but with the *right support* you'll make it.

Make sure you aren't drowning yourself with work. You
will lose creativity if you don't take breaks and enjoy life. I hit
a writing slump once and put my manuscript away for a day
and went to visit a friend. The next day I was refreshed and
my mind was reeling with ideas and information that was just
waiting to be written down…seriously.

-Stay Focused.

Distraction is one of the toughest hurdles when you're a
writer; with all the pressures of building your platform,
establishing personal connections, etc. Bottom line: you can't
be a writer unless you're writing. I got caught up in this
myself; guilty as charged. It took me twice as long to finish
the sequel to my second romance novel as it did the first
book. I was working on promoting my second memoir at the
time. It's really tough to stay balanced when you're working
on a book and trying to promote another. But the truth is
that *the best way to keep promoting your books is to write and
publish another.* I'm sure you've heard that before. It's true.

It's also tough to keep writing books when you're *constantly
writing blogs.* This is my paramount issue. I try to post a blog
five days a week. Sometimes I do it. Sometimes I don't. The
only advantage I have is that I have two completed
manuscripts (one edited) under my belt. But it also takes me
twice as long to write a book now!

-Exercise

I've said it before and I'll say it again: there's something about exercising that brings out the best in us. When I exercise it's like I'm getting in touch with myself. It's more than just exercise; it's centering your thoughts, clearing your mind, de-stressing, cleansing your body and energizing. Those endorphins…they aren't a myth, trust me! Do you know how many positive thoughts and ideas I've had during exercise? You probably wouldn't believe me if I told you.

I follow all these steps and I've written eight books, published six, have two works in progress, and my 'idea diary' if you will, has approximately ten more book ideas sitting there just waiting to be written.

Don't Get Stuck in the Promotional Time Warp

How much time do you spend promoting your work? How much is too much?
It's really tough to find the correct balance, especially when you have underlying factors to contend with like work (paid work that is), family time and whatever other personal endeavours you have in your life.

In the beginning, I spent all my time writing and nothing on promotion. This netted me zero sales for my first two books. Then I did what all newbie authors do (at least those who aren't in the know like I was) and promoted the heck out of my second book AFTER its release.

What I know now and what I wish I knew then, is that I needed to establish my platform BEFORE releasing my book.

Hence the problem: how much promotion is enough?

Some of the blogs I've read in the past year say you should spend 80% of your time writing and 20% promoting. I can tell you that this is a tough ratio to maintain and I'd love to say that I spent 80% of my time writing, but I'd be lying.

When I began promoting my first romance novel, I can honestly say I did little else. Luckily by then my second romance novel was already finished, it just needed editing. Where I got stuck was in creating my platform and promoting my first novel, when in reality I should have been promoting my second novel.

I think it's not so much HOW MUCH TIME we spend promoting, it's the TIMING of the promotion.

I considered hiring a publicist to do some promotion for me, and in doing research; I realized that some publicists recommend starting the promotional campaign for a book at least six months in advance. What does this tell us? You guessed it; we need to start promoting our book about six months before its release.

This is very bad news, since most authors start promoting only a month or two before their book is to be released (myself included).

Does this mean wait to release it? I think absolutely not. Why? Because if you've already begun promoting it, this will hurt your credibility.

I consider it a lesson learned, and I'll make sure the promotional campaign for my next book starts well in advance of its release. One thing I recommend is to include the first chapter or an excerpt from your next novel at the end of your current release. I did this with both my romances and it does help to create interest.

Here's another point: there are so many promotional avenues available that we get stuck. We spend more time surfing the net for various promotional sites and ways to get noticed that we aren't productive anymore.
Here's what I have to say about that: Don't get stuck in the promotional time warp!

I'm guilty. I totally did it. I got stuck many times. What do I do to steer clear?
I do my writing FIRST.

I check my emails, Facebook, Twitter, etc. AFTER

I recommend that you don't even log into the internet. Open Word and go!
Remember: the internet is ADDICTIVE, especially when you're getting responses from blog posts, new likes and friend requests, etc. etc. etc. These all feed our egos and get us into trouble!

I know it's important to respond to these things, but there is a time to do it; AFTER you've written something. After all, what's the point in developing a huge writing platform if at the end of the day you've got nothing more to publish! Eek!

If you want some great advice on establishing your platform, I recommend reading Chuck Sambuchino's 'Create Your Writer Platform' it was very helpful; I wish I'd read it sooner.

Conclusion

Just like anything else in life, if writing makes you happy, do it. Sometimes it gets overwhelming with all the new information available and with trying to figure out which course of action is best for you to take. Go with your gut instinct. If something doesn't feel right, isn't working for you or costs too much money; try something else.

The other thing is to make sure you have a good support system both within your platform and at home. Your online friends, if they're good ones, will guide you through and give you helpful advice without asking for anything in return. At home it's equally important to have a healthy support system because without it, how will you ever find the time or inspiration to write?

You've probably read how fast the publishing industry is changing and all different opinions on traditional publishers, indie writers and the clash between the two. The most important thing to remember is that like life, being an author is turbulent; just hang in there and do what you feel is best for you; everything else will fall into place.

If you need more help establishing your online platform, please check out the mate to this book, called 'How to Get Followers on Twitter'. Simply put, it's all the tips and ideas I used to help me gain a decent following. No gimmicks.

I hope you enjoyed this book and I wish you all the luck with your writing career.

Now Available! Indie Writing Advice Volume II!

INDIE WRITING ADVICE

A Simple Guide for Sharpening Your Writing Skills,
Platform Building, and Submitting to Publishers

DENICE SHAW

Click this link to purchase
http://www.amazon.com/dp/B00J7YSLI8

Also check out!

HOW TO GET FOLLOWERS ON TWITTER

A Simple Guide on How to
Optimize Twitter and Hootsuite

DENICE SHAW

Click this link to purchase:
http://www.amazon.com/dp/B00CEJGM9I

www.ingramcontent.com/pod-product-compliance
Lightning Source LLC
Chambersburg PA
CBHW071633170526
45166CB00003B/1316